KABBALAH

FOR

EVANGELICAL CHRISTIANS

Alfred D. Byrd

KABBALAH FOR EVANGELICAL CHRISTIANS

ISBN 978-0-6151-6440-3

Books published by Lulu Enterprises
may be ordered on line at

www.lulu.com

INTRODUCTION

Kabbalah means 'tradition.' The word refers to mystical Jewish teachings on the deep things of God.

Some of these teachings were already around in the time of Jesus Christ. In the New Testament, our Savior and Lord and His Apostles dealt with issues arising from these teachings.

Much of modern Kabbalah, though, originated in the Twelfth Century in what's now Spain, and developed further in the Sixteenth Century in the Holy Land. This form of Kabbalah came down to our time through **Hasidic Jews**, ultra-Orthodox Jews from Eastern Europe whose religion is highly emotional and mystical.

For centuries the teachings of Kabbalah were largely kept secret from Gentiles and even from most Jews. Rabbis trained in Kabbalah (**Kabbalists**) deemed knowledge of it dangerous to ignorant persons. Kabbalists tell a story of four rabbis who entered the orchard of Paradise (that is, reached mystical enlightenment). One of the rabbis died of his experience, one of them went mad from it, and a third became a heretic. Only the fourth received true light.

During the centuries of secrecy, Kabbalists handed down their knowledge of the deep things only to persons who met five standards. Such persons had to be:

- men
- trained as rabbis in Torah and Talmud
- at least forty years old
- married
- the father of at least three children

The Kabbalists believed that only such persons might be stable enough to learn the deep things without going mad or falling into heresy.

When the New Age Movement began, though, some Kabbalists decided to make the secret tradition commonly available. They believed that the time of **Messiah** (the anointed deliverer promised in Hebrew Scripture, whom we Evangelical Christians identify as Jesus Christ) was near, and that making the secret tradition public would speed his coming. Thus, we now have such previously unlikely Kabbalists as Demi Moore and Madonna.

Such persons seek what traditional Kabbalists have sought:

- an explanation of the nature of creation,
- an explanation of the individual's relationship to both creation and its Creator, and
- a spiritual union with the ultimate God

deeper than what traditional religion can give them. Such persons seek to climb Jacob's ladder from the everyday world of human darkness rooted in spiritual ignorance to the ultimate world of divine light rooted in spiritual knowledge. The quest for spiritual enlightenment through knowledge of deep things links Kabbalah to the New Age.

Still, though Kabbalah has become part of the New Age, Kabbalah's roots are old. As you'll learn, you may well have met many Kabbalistic concepts in your everyday life, even if you hadn't heard of Kabbalah till now. These concepts may even be part of your faith and practice as an Evangelical Christian.

In these days, when we meet ideas of many religions, we need to know what's authentically part of our own faith and practice. Thus, as I tell you of Kabbalah, I'll compare and contrast the principles of Jewish mysticism with the principles of Evangelical Christianity that lead us to a saving knowledge of our Savior and Lord, Jesus Christ, and enable us to live in a way that glorifies God.

Kabbalah and Evangelical Christianity are widely misunderstood fields of beliefs that tend to misunderstand each other. I hope that by presenting both fields of belief fairly in this book I'll help relieve the misunderstanding of both fields of faith.

Chapter One

A BRIEF HISTORY OF KABBALAH

Early Jewish Mysticism: Chariot, Temple, Creation

As I said earlier, some of the ideas that make up modern Kabbalah were already around in the time of our Savior and Lord. These grew in complexity during the first few centuries of the Roman Empire. Some Jewish scholars, perhaps influenced by mystery religions of Babylon, Egypt, Greece, and India, became mystics, seeking direct experience of God's Presence. This experience, they sought through three pathways.

The first was seeking visions of the **merkavah**, the chariot in which God rides. This appears in the account of the Prophet Elijah's being taken to the heavens in a whirlwind, but most famously in the visions of the Prophet Ezekiel in Babylonian exile. These are the visions that some New Agers have called Biblical "proof" of the existence of flying saucers.

These New Agers were not the first mystics to attach outrageous explanations to Ezekiel's prophecies. The accounts that Jewish mystics wrote of their vision of the Chariot were so fantastic and so seemingly heretical that many rabbis, to safeguard the faith of ordinary Jews, forbade them to study Ezekiel's visions.

The second pathway was seeking visions of the **heikhal**, the heavenly temple of which God's temple in Jerusalem was just an earthly copy. In mystical visions, the Holy of Holies, which in the earthly temple once held the Ark of the Covenant, was God's throne room. There nine (or more) choirs of angels surrounded Him. Mystical accounts of visions of the *heikhal* include elaborate descriptions and measurements of the throne room, the angels, and God Himself.

The most famous such account is **Shi'ur Komah,** 'The Measurement of the Heights.' This starts with a description of God as an anthropomorphic (human-shaped) being of fabulous dimensions, but goes on to reveal that God's smallest dimension is larger than the universe. The true lesson of the work is not that God has a human form, but that God, in His full divinity, is beyond the power of humans to grasp.

The third pathway was seeking visions of **bereshit**, the creation of the heavens and the earth. **Sefer Yetzirah**, *The Book of Formation*, describes in incredibly *abstruse* (difficult and hidden) language how God created all things by means of thirty-two "channels," the twenty-two Hebrew letters and the ten numbers, or **sefirot**.

I'll say much more of letters and numbers later. *Sefer Yetzirah*, though, is foundational to the rest of Kabbalah. Because the book implied that the creative power of letters and numbers was available, not only to God, but also to enlightened humans, *Sefer Yetzirah* became the first basis of Kabbalistic magic, which I'll discuss at this book's end.

A fusion of the three schools of mysticism produced elaborate accounts of the origin of the seven levels of the heavens, angels, and humanity. Such accounts appear in a number of ancient texts, of which **The Book of Enoch** is the most famous. This work details a celestial journey of the Patriarch Enoch, who Scripture implies did not die, but was taken by God from the earth.

According to the Book of Enoch, at the end of his journey Enoch encounters the archangel **Metatron**. This name comes from the Greek phrase ***meta thronou***, 'beside the throne.' In Jewish mystical literature, Metatron stands beside God's throne and often speaks as His agent, or as God Himself. The account of Enoch's visions has been preserved in a number of editions in a variety of ancient languages.

The Beginnings of Modern Kabbalah

The mysticism of *merkavah, heikhal,* and *bereshit* was controversial in the Jewish community. This mysticism largely died out in centuries of persecution that Jews endured in the Roman Empire, first from pagans, and then from those who called themselves Christians, but took God's authority of judgment upon themselves. This form of mysticism seemed too individualistic and dangerous to a Jewish community that needed a strong ethical basis to survive persecution.

A new school of Jewish mysticism, though, related to the first, arose in Spain in the Twelfth Century. Spain was then ruled by moderate Sunni Moslems who allowed religious freedom. Thus, Spain became a meeting place for Roman Catholics from Western Europe, Orthodox Christians from Eastern Europe, Moslems, and Jews.

In Spain also, and in Provence, in southern France, were offshoots of an ancient religious movement called **Gnosticism.** This taught that matter is evil, and only spirit is good. Gnostics believe that the world in which we live as sparks of spirit trapped in material bodies is separated by many spiritual planes from the One True God.

The freewheeling atmosphere of Spain and Provence sparked a new form of Jewish mysticism. This used the Gnostic concept of a changeless God separated from creation by a number of spiritual planes. This new form of mysticism, its practitioners called Kabbalah, for they said that it was an ancient tradition handed down ultimately from Abraham and Moses.

The secrets of Kabbalah were handed down by word of mouth directly from master to student. Allusions to the secrets, though, were recorded in a number of texts. The first of these is **Sefer Ha-Bahir**, *The Book of Brightness.* This book, of unknown authorship and antiquity, was first published in the Twelfth Century, but was attributed to a rabbi of the First Century.

Sefer ha-Bahir expands on the thirty-two paths of creation by giving the first complete description of the ten *sefirot* and the first clear explanation of the Jewish doctrine of reincarnation. Many other ideas foundational to modern Kabbalah first appear in *Sefer ha-Bahir.*

The most famous Kabbalistic text, and in many ways the most important commentary on Kabbalah, is **Sefer Ha-Zohar**, *The Book of Splendor.* Usually you'll hear it called simply *The Zohar.* This is a mystical commentary on the five books of Moses. Interspersed with commentary is a set of parables, amounting to almost a complete history, of the mystical journeys of a group of rabbis living around the time of Christ.

Early on, *The Zohar* got a reputation in Kabbalistic circles of having a holiness next only to that of canonical Hebrew Scripture. Kabbalists traditionally ascribe *The Zohar* to one of the early rabbis, but most modern scholars deem it the work, at least in part, of a Twelfth-Century Spanish Kabbalist, **Rabbi Moses de Leon**.

Lurianic Kabbalah

The form of Kabbalah that arose in Moslem Spain spread throughout the Jewish world and is the direct ancestor of modern Kabbalah. For centuries masters handed down secrets to students and recorded new speculations on Kabbalah in a bewildering variety of texts.

Kabbalah survived because, by giving Jews an explanation of sin and suffering in a fallen world that's just the gateway to the world of glory, Kabbalah helped the Jewish community survive persecution by those who called themselves Christians, but sometimes showed the fruit of servants of Satan. As one noted rabbi of the Eighteenth Century would say, "I daily thank God for not having been born before *The Zohar* was revealed, for it's *The Zohar* that's upheld me in my faith as a Jew."

Kabbalah took a new direction in the Sixteenth Century. In a town called Safed in the Holy Land, then part of the Ottoman Empire, lived a community of Kabbalists. An Egyptian Jew, **Rabbi Isaac Luria**, came to Safed to learn from the Kabbalists, but stayed there to become their greatest teacher.

In his brief lifetime Rabbi Luria radically transformed Kabbalah with the teaching that, by keeping the commandments of the Law of Moses, Jews could heal a fallen creation and repair the breach between God and humanity. The healing and repair would take place when devout Jews, by righteous acts, freed sparks of God's creative light that had been trapped in a fallen world when the vessels holding the light had shattered.

Rabbi Luria didn't write down his own ideas, but his students recorded them in a wide array of Kabbalistic works. As it's mainly Lurianic Kabbalah that I'll discuss in this book, I'll say no more of Rabbi Luria's teachings now.

Shabbetai Zevi: False Messiah

In the Seventeenth Century a Jew influenced by Rabbi Luria's ideas caused one of the greatest scandals in Jewish history. This Jew, called **Shabbetai Zevi**, claimed to be the promised Messiah who'd restore to the Jews the Holy Land in the extent promised to Abraham.

Shabbetai Zevi was upheld in this claim by a respected Kabbalist named **Nathan of Gaza,** who was in some ways to Shabbetai Zevi what John the Baptist was to Jesus. In the eyes of some Jews, Nathan was a forerunner Messiah, *Messiah ben Joseph,* to Shabbetai Zevi's completed Messiah, *Messiah ben David.*

Shabbetai Zevi led a movement that swept like wildfire through the Jewish world. He proclaimed, among many other beliefs outrageous to Orthodox Jewish thought, that Jews, by undergoing rigorous penances, could ensure Messiah's coming in the fateful year of 1666 by the Christian calendar. (Some Christian mystics had previously predicted this year as the time for Christ's Second Coming on the basis of the year's containing the numeral 666, the mystical number of the Beast who'd oppose God at the end of the Age of the Church.)

Many Jews, at the so-called Messiah's urging, did such bizarre and traditionally non-Jewish acts as fasting to the point of human endurance, lying naked in snow, and whipping themselves mercilessly. Shabbetai Zevi seemed on the verge of leading his people to the Holy Land when he was captured by the Ottoman Sultan, Sunni Islam's spiritual and political head at the time.

In captivity Shabbetai Zevi converted to Islam. Most of his followers, disillusioned by his apostasy from Judaism, deserted him. A few fanatical followers, though, sought in Kabbalistic interpretations of Biblical texts an explanation why Messiah had to become a Moslem.

These Kabbalists taught that Shabbetai Zevi had just pretended to convert to Islam so that he could free sparks of light trapped in Moslem lands. When Shabbetai Zevi died without having renounced Islam, his followers taught that he'd just gone into hiding till a time planned by God. These followers persisted for centuries and occasionally produced other outbursts of Messianic fervor. Shabbetaian Kabbalah lies behind, or at least contributed to, some forms of modern occultism.

An Aside on Jewish Messianism

Shabbetai Zevi hasn't been the only Jewish claimant to be Messiah. The most famous would-be Messiah is **Simon bar Kochba** ['Son of the Star']. He lived early in the Second Century, about fifty years after the destruction of Herod's Temple. Urged by **Rabbi Akiva**, the time's foremost Jewish religious authority, to proclaim himself Messiah, bar Kochba led an ill-fated rebellion of the Holy Land's Jews against the pagan Roman emperor, **Hadrian**.

Although bar Kochba apparently fulfilled Messiah's role in Jewish Messianic thought by briefly rebuilding the Temple, his revolt ended in disaster. Perhaps a million Jews died at Roman hands. Jerusalem was again destroyed, and Hadrian barred Jews from returning to its site for centuries to come.

There've been several other Jewish claimants to be Messiah, but none of them has had anything like the influence of Simon bar Kochba and Shabbetai Zevi. The most recent Jewish candidate to be Messiah was **Rabbi Menachem Mendel Schneerson**, head of the Lubavitcher community of Hasidic Jews in New York City.

Rabbi Schneerson himself never directly claimed to be Messiah, but many of his followers have claimed so for him. Even though the rabbi has died, some of his followers claim to this day that he never truly died, but is waiting to come to Jerusalem to rebuild the temple and reign over the Holy Land in righteousness and peace. In his day, Rabbi Schneerson was the head of a significant movement of Kabbalistic Jews.

Baal Shem Tov and the Hasidic Movement

Shabbetai Zevi gave Kabbalah a bad odor to much of the Jewish community, which was anyway largely turning to rational ideas of the Enlightenment. Kabbalah, though, found a new lease on life in Eastern Europe. There **Hasidic Jews**, marked by their black clothing and their men's sidelocks and broad-brimmed hats, kept the movement alive for the future.

The spiritual founder of the Hasidic Jews was Rabbi Israel, who went by the title **Baal Shem Tov**, 'master of the good name.' Building on Luria's work, the Baal Shem Tov taught the concept of the **tzaddik**, 'the righteous one.' This person keeps the world in existence by devotedly performing God's commandments with the intention of healing creation.

As the doctrine of the *tzaddik* developed, ten *tzaddikim* had to be living in the world at all times to keep it from God's destruction in judgment. The requirement for ten *tzaddikim* is linked to the **minyan**, the requirement that ten adult Jewish men be present in a synagogue for full services to take place there.

Both requirements go back to the Scriptural account in which Abraham won God's consent not to destroy the wicked cites of Sodom and Gomorrah if ten righteous men were there, but God destroyed the cities anyway because they held too few righteous persons.

The *tzaddikim* became judges and spiritual leaders of Hasidic communities, and often passed their authority down to their sons. The work of healing the world, though, wasn't just for *tzaddikim*, but for every Jew in the Hasidic communities. Hasidic worship is an ecstatic experience in which sacred dance may give one heavenly visions. It's not wholly inaccurate to refer to Hasidic Jews as Pentecostal Jews.

Non-Jewish "Kabbalists"

Let me pause here to point out that Kabbalah spread to some non-Jews as early as the Reformation. These were Christian mystics who combined often mistaken ideas of Kabbalah with Christian mysticism to form a so-called Christian Cabala. This blends a traditional Christian mystic's quest to become one with God's light with "magic" (literally, the lore of the Magi) containing elements of Kabbalah and alchemy.

Later, in the Nineteenth Century, occultists studying ancient Egyptian and Greek systems of magic combined these with Kabbalistic lore to form the so-called Hermetic Qabalah. Note the spelling of Kabbalah unique to each of these systems. As they lie beyond this book's scope, I'll say no more of them, but if you come across the names you'll know what's going on.

Recent Developments in Kabbalah

In the Nineteenth Century, Jews began to return in large numbers to the Holy Land. There the existing Kabbalistic communities were joined by colonies of Hasidic Jews bringing new ideas from Eastern Europe. Under a number of prominent rabbis, of whom the most famous is **Abraham Isaac Kook**, the Kabbalists of the Holy Land began to develop the idea that devotion to doing God's commandments could speed Messiah's coming.

In time, when the New Age movement became prominent, some of the rabbis influenced by Rabbi Kook accepted the idea that women and even Gentiles could take part in the work of speeding Messiah's coming. Although the simplified Kabbalah taught by some of these rabbis, with its emphasis on chanting the Seventy-Two Names of God, wearing the red string, and using Kabbalah water, is controversial among traditional Kabbalists, it's proving popular in the world at large.

Praise for a Great Scholar of Kabbalah

I can't end this section without mentioning the inestimable debt that the study of Kabbalah owes to **Professor Gershom Scholem**, a German Jew who made a life's work of learning Kabbalah's origin and history. Professor Scholem preserved and studied many ancient Kabbalistic manuscripts that would else have been lost in the Holocaust.

His writings on Kabbalah set a standard for scholarship that makes them still well worth reading today. Although he wasn't himself a Kabbalist, his influence on Kabbalah is equal to that of many of the greatest Kabbalists.

Chapter Two

THE SACRED TEXT OF KABBALAH

In the preceding section I mentioned a number of books. These, according to Kabbalists, contain, not new knowledge, but oral traditions handed down to the present through Jewish scholars from such important figures in Judaism as the Patriarchs Enoch, Noah, Abraham, and Moses, as well as the rabbis who lived around the time of Christ. These books form just the foundation of an immense body of Kabbalistic literature, which is more than a lifetime's study for any Kabbalist.

All of this literature, though, is just commentary on Kabbalah's true holy book, the Bible. Specifically, Kabbalists believe that the **Torah,** the collection of five books attributed to Moses, is a repository of hidden knowledge.

Kabbalists would agree with us Evangelical Christians on the Torah when we say, "God moved prophets through the Holy Spirit to give revelations that are authoritative for faith and practice."

Kabbalists, though, go further than most of us when they say that the very letters of the Torah, and indeed the very shapes of the letters, are divinely inspired. Kabbalists teach that Hebrew letters form a kind of toolkit that God used to create the heavens and the earth. Some Kabbalists teach that God first created the Torah as letters of black fire on white fire; then He studied the Torah for two thousand years before He created anything else.

Indeed, some Kabbalists have such an exalted view of the Torah that they identify it with God Himself, almost as what we'd call an incarnation.

In the eyes of the Kabbalists, Torah has

- an outward (*exoteric*) meaning that anyone can learn, and
- an inward (*esoteric*) meaning that only a Kabbalist can learn.

Kabbalists have claimed to learn this inward meaning through a variety of techniques, including study of Scripture, prayer, fasting, meditation, and sacred dance. Much of Kabbalistic teaching, though, comes from one special Kabbalistic technique that has been in the news lately, but has generally been misunderstood. I'll discuss this technique in the next chapter.

Chapter Three

A BASIC TECHNIQUE OF KABBALAH

Kabbalists have claimed to learn the inward, hidden meaning of the Torah through an esoteric science called **Gematria**, the study of the mystical meaning of Hebrew letters. (The Hebrew word *gematria* apparently comes from the same Greek word that gives us the English word *geometry.)* Gematria is not a single technique, but a set of techniques, all based on the concept that Hebrew letters form the toolkit that God used to create the heavens and the earth.

The Science of Shapes

One technique of Gematria is meditation on the shapes of the Hebrew letters. These have, in Kabbalistic reasoning, not have accidental shapes developed by humans, but divinely planned shapes carrying deep meanings and profound power. Through learning the mystical meanings of these shapes, Kabbalists claim, one gains deep insights into God's mind.

The Science of Numbers

A second technique depends on the ancient Jews' having used Hebrew letters as numbers. By converting each letter of a Hebrew word into its equivalent numerical value, adding the values of the letters together, and finding other words with equal numerical values, Kabbalists can find relationships between words that are mystically linked by numerical equivalence.

Kabbalists say that, since Hebrew is the language that God created, and spoke when He created the heavens and the earth, it can't be a coincidence that two words in Hebrew have the same numerical value. Thus, Hebrew words are linked through their numerical values into families. Each member of a family of words is linked to other members of its family in mystical meaning.

The Kabbalists are using a basic principle of Aristotelian logic, "Things that are equal to equal things are equal to each other." By this principle, Kabbalists can show that words, phrases, and even whole passages of Scripture that on the surface are unrelated actually refer to the same thing.

(Some Evangelical Christians, your author among them, have wasted time in using the second technique of Gematria to try to identify the coming Antichrist from the number of the Beast, 666. We've generally done Gematria on Greek letters, not on Hebrew, but the technique for both languages is the same. Shame on me, and may God guide everyone else away from the futile pastime of trying to identify the Antichrist by mystical means!)

The Science of Vowels

A third technique of Gematria is finding new meanings in the Torah by changing the vowels written above and below its consonants. This technique is legitimate in Kabbalists' eyes because the Torah's original text consisted only of consonants. Vowel marks were added by Jewish scholars called the Masoretes more than a millennium after the texts were first written down.

If I may give an absurd example from English, this technique is equivalent to saying that the words *ban, bean, bin, bone,* and *bun* are all equivalent because they consist of the same consonants in the same order. To Kabbalists, though, the technique is legitimate because the Hebrew language is the direct creation of God, Who allows no coincidence.

The Science of Anagrams

If words with equal numerical values are equivalent to each other, then all words with the same consonants must belong to the same family of words. Thus, a fourth technique of Gematria is to find new meanings in the Torah by changing the order of consonants in a word of text. (Shame on my Evangelical Christian brothers and sisters who at this point are saying, "Doesn't that make *God* equivalent to *dog*?"!)

The Science of Matrices

As you might've guessed, the three preceding techniques make it possible for Kabbalists to find an infinite constellation of meanings in the Torah. Indeed, some Kabbalists go as far as to teach that the Torah has no one outward meaning, but is really just an expression of the unknowable Name of God, in which all true meaning is hidden.

Some Kabbalists teach, too, that the Torah had one, original meaning when God created it in His throne room, took on a second, temporal meaning when creation fell into spiritual darkness, and will take on a third, completed meaning when Messiah comes. By their reasoning the Torah's commandments are temporary, limited provisions for freeing a fallen world from spiritual darkness. These will be replaced, when Messiah comes, with eternal, perfect commandments for an age of righteousness and peace.

The teaching that the Torah has an infinite constellation of meanings has given rise to a fifth technique of Gematria. This consists of writing texts from the Torah in matrices (grids) and finding new meanings in words that appear up and down or diagonally in the grids. You may've heard of this technique as the **Bible Code.** Many of my Evangelical Christian brothers and sisters have been carried away by this. To them I say, "Believe in the Bible Code only if you believe everything else that Gematria can teach you."

In any case, it's from Gematria and from kindred techniques of mediation and Bible study that Kabbalists have leaned the once-secret doctrines that I'll discuss in the following sections.

Chapter Four

THE ULTIMATE GOD OF KABBALAH

The secret doctrines begin with God.

Kabbalists believe, like us, that in the beginning there was nothing but God, Who

- has existed from eternity past,
- is complete in Himself, and
- is beyond human understanding.

We call this God (The Father) *transcendent*, meaning 'above and beyond everything else.'

Kabbalists call Him ***Ein Sof***, 'the without limit.' They say that He so far transcends us that He has no attributes that have anything in common with what we perceive with our senses. In fact, our senses only impede our getting in touch with Ein Sof. He exists without time, without space, without change, and without feeling in a realm completely apart from our world of motion and decay. He is best described in terms of what He is not, for what is He is is unlike what we are. In a word, Ein Sof is *incomprehensible*.

The words *transcendent* and *incomprehensible* have tremendous implications for our relationship with God. These words point out to us that we, as finite creatures limited to the here and now, can never truly understand the One Whom we're trying to understand. We can use only human words, slippery in definition, to speak of the One Who is anyway beyond definition. The words *transcendent* and *incomprehensible* point out to us that, in the light of eternity and infinity, we're helpless, unable to reach the God Who Is.

If God is transcendent and incomprehensible, how can He relate to human beings? Is God forever apart from and unconcerned with us, or does He somehow reach out of transcendence to touch us in our everyday lives? Is He also somehow *immanent,* God With Us, in a way that we can understand?

Both Kabbalah and Evangelical Christianity answer the last question "yes." The two schools of faith and practice, though, disagree on how God reaches out.

We say that God sent His Son (Jesus Christ) into the world to live a perfect human life and open the way to the Father,

and the Holy Spirit into the world to live within each of us believers and bind us together as the Body of Christ with Jesus as its head.

Kabbalists have quite a different belief from ours. It has, though, like ours, three parts: Creation, the Fall, and Redemption. Through comparing and contrasting Evangelical Christian beliefs with Kabbalistic beliefs on the three sections of the Story of God with Humanity, we'll learn much of the once-secret tradition that's making many converts today, and maybe we'll come to understand our own faith and practice better.

Chapter Five

CREATION ACCORDING TO KABBALAH

According to theologians, there are three ways in which God could've created the heavens and the earth.

ONE: Physical matter came into being separately from God. He just organized it into the world that now is.

The belief that matter arose as a sea of *chaos* (disorder) is the belief once held by the Babylonians and the ancient Egyptians. It is also held by some Modernist Christians.
You can find it clearly explained by Rabbi Harold S. Kushner in *Why Bad Things Happen to Good People*. According to him, God isn't truly *omnipotent* (able to do all things), as God didn't create matter, but was forced to work with matter already present. God, though, can still be *omnibenevolent* (wishing good for everyone). The bad things that happen to us are not God's fault, but come about because of matter's limitations.

TWO: We believe that God made everything out of nothing. (Fancy-schmantzy Evangelical Christian preachers and teachers like to show off by using the Latin phrase ***creatio ex nihil***, 'creation out of nothing.') We interpret the creation account of Genesis One to mean that God spoke, and what had never been came to be. Thus, only God existed till He said, "Let there be light!"

According to Creatio ex Nihil, only God is independent and transcendent; everything else is dependent and *contingent* (existing because of something else that happened in the past). In other words, God is the only true **Being** (that which exists in itself); everything else is just a **creature** (that which exists because something else made it.) We see this truth in the name **I Am** that God gave Moses in the *theophany* (appearance of God's Presence) at the burning bush.

THREE: Kabbalists teach that, since Ein Sof filled everything, nothing besides Ein Sof can exist. Thus, He must've made everything out of Himself. A Latin phrase for this teaching is **creatio ex Se**, 'creation out of Himself.'

The Kabbalistic teaching is at least **panentheism**, the concept that God is intrinsically part of everything that exists. Some schools of Kabbalah may reach the level of **pantheism**, the concept that God is everything, and everything is God. In pantheism there's ultimately no difference between Creator and creation. I'll explore some of the implications of Creatio ex Se in later chapters.

There are many Kabbalistic accounts of how God created the heavens and the earth out of Himself. The currently most popular account was first fully explained by Rabbi Luria in the Sixteenth Century and has been passed down from the Hasidic Jews to the New Age. I'll give you a simplified explanation of this account in the following chapters.

Chapter Six

THE SPIRITUAL PLANES OF KABBALAH

Since God filled everything, Rabbi Luria taught that He had to withdraw to make empty space where other things could exist. The process of withdrawal or contraction is called *tsimtsum*. As God contracted, He left behind Him ten empty shells or vessels. These are commonly called *Sefirot*, a word that in different contexts means 'numbers,' 'upper worlds,' or 'spiritual planes.' These ten vessels, He then filled with His light. Thus, all things consist of vessels holding God's light.

(Anyone who's read Lurianic works knows that I've radically simplified, or maybe even oversimplified, Rabbi Luria's teachings. Please keep in mind that this is a book for persons with no previous knowledge of Kabbalah.)

Each of the ten Sefirot (I'll use the term 'Planes' from here on out) has its own set of names, along with its distinctive manifestation of God and set of angels who serve that manifestation. From highest to lowest, the Planes are:

CROWN (*keter*) the highest Plane, closest to Ein Sof. This is the home of the masculine, rational manifestation of God known by the name *Ehyeh*, "I Am." Crown is also known as *ayin*, the nothingness out of which all else emerged.

WISDOM (*hochma*) the first point of creation that emanates (flows out) from the primordial nothingness. The name of God associated with wisdom is *YHWH*, the sacred name of God that devout Jews do not pronounce. I'll say more on this name later.

UNDERSTANDING (*binah*) the womb from which the seed of Wisdom gave rise to the lower seven Planes. Understanding is sometimes also called *teshuvah*, 'return,' for it's the "place" to which a seeker of enlightenment must come to find the Divine wisdom and ultimately be dissolved in the nothingness from which all else arose.

KINDNESS (*hesed*) the first of a pair of attributes that, perfectly balanced, give rise to the Beauty of a life of happiness pleasing to God.

STRENGTH (*gevurah*) Kindness's necessary counterpart, which prevents us from falling into the nightmare world of permissiveness that would arise if we followed Aleister Crowley's teaching, "Do as thou wilt shall be the whole of the law." A nightmare world of oppression, though, results if Strength is unbalanced by Mercy. Strength is also known as *Din*, 'judgment.'

BEAUTY (*tif'eret*) the balanced life that results from the fruitful cooperation of Mercy and Strength. Kabbalists consider Beauty the center of the other nine Planes. They also call it *Rahamim*, 'compassion,' and *Emet*, 'truth.' The name of God associated with Beauty is *Ha-Qodesh Barukh Hu,* "The Holy One, Blessed Be He."

VICTORY (*netzah*) the right-side pathway of prophecy and the Messiah.

AWE (*hod*) the left-side pathway of submission and service to God.

FOUNDATION (*yesod*) a balance of holy zeal and holy humility. Foundation is associated with the Jewish rite of circumcision as creative energy brought into subjection to God's will. Foundation is the Plane from which the forces of the higher planes flow into the lowest. Another name for Foundation is *tzaddik*, 'the righteous one.'

KINGDOM (*malchuth*) the lowest Plane, farthest from Ein Sof. This is our home, as well as the home of the feminine, emotional manifestation of God, **Shekhinah**, the Daughter of Understanding and the Bride of Beauty, the origin of the human soul and the gateway to Ein Sof.

The ten Planes may be represented in a number of forms. Sometimes, Kabbalists draw them in a circle that begins and ends with Crown. Sometimes, Kabbalists draw the ten Planes in the form of the Tree of Life from the Garden of Eden.

Most significantly, the Kabbalists draw the ten Planes as **Adam Kadmon**, a cosmic man who manifests Ein Sof's hidden nature in creation. On Adam Kadmon, Crown is the head, Kingdom appears as the feet, Mercy is the right hand, and Judgment is the left.

By the principle of "As above, so below," Kabbalists see the earthly Adam and each of us who is descended from him as a manifestation in the lowest realm of the cosmic man in the highest realm. I'll say more of this principle in the sections on works of righteousness and magic.

If you go on to read the works that I list in Bibliography, you'll learn that the story of the ten Planes may be far more complicated than I've described to you. Some Kabbalists believe that the ten Planes exist within four spiritual worlds of emanation. The highest of these is **Atsilut** ("Linkage"), where God Himself lives in unapproachable glory. Below this world is **Beri'ah** ("creation"); below this, **Yetzirah** ("formation"); below this, **Asiyah** ("doing"), the world in which we live.

Each of the three lowest worlds holds a set of the ten Planes. Kabbalists envision these worlds and their Planes as a ladder like the one that the Patriarch Jacob saw in his vision of God at Bethel. Kabbalists strive mystically to climb this ladder so that they can achieve a spiritual union with God in the ultimate world of *Atsilut*.

Some Kabbalists complicate the picture further by teaching that nested within each of the three sets of ten Planes in the three lowest worlds is a further set of Planes, so that there are actually hundreds of Planes between human beings and God. I'll say no more of this teaching, as it lies beyond this book's scope.

Chapter Seven

A SERMON ON THE TEN PLANES AND THE TRINITY

Sometimes, Christians who learn of the ten Planes react to them by saying, "If Jews believe that God is Ein Sof Who manifests Himself in ten Planes, why do Jews criticize us for believing that that God is one Nature in three Persons?" This question reflects misunderstanding on the part of both Christians and Jews of what Planes and Persons are.

As I said earlier, Kabbalah derives some of its teachings from an earlier mystical religious movement called Gnosticism. The ten Planes owe something to Gnostic teachings on **emanations**. This is an imposing word that simply means "outflowings."

According to Gnostics, the ultimate God is a perfect, self-contained, unknowable unity of spirit who is too holy to have anything to do with the world of matter, which is filled with evil. God, the Gnostics say, didn't create the universe directly; instead, many levels of spiritual realms emanated from God. Each successive realm was filled with gods who held less and less of God's light.

At length there arose a realm so far from him that it held the **Demiurge**, a god who was so blind that he committed the ultimate sin of creating matter and trapping within it pure spirit. Gnostics of Jewish and Christian origin often identified this creator god with the God of the Book of Genesis.

Kabbalists, like Gnostics, believe that Ein Sof is a perfect, self-contained, unknowable unity of spirit infinitely above the physical world, from which He is separated by many spiritual Planes. Unlike the Gnostics, though, the Kabbalists believe that Ein Sof is the creator of the physical world, which He made good, and which fell into evil for reasons that I'll discuss later.

Gnostics believed that the emanations and the physical world are almost accidental in origin; Kabbalists believe that Ein Sof deliberately created the ten Planes as vessels through with divine light could flow to the physical world.

Emanations and Planes sound strange to us Evangelical Christians, who learn the belief that God created the world directly through His Word (in our thought, the pre-incarnate Son), and that we're connected with God directly through the Holy Spirit and the Son. What, then, if anything, do Emanations and Planes have to do with Persons of the Trinity?

"Nothing at all!" said the Church Fathers who defined the doctrine of the Trinity. They lived in a world in which Gnosticism flourished, and were careful to say that the Persons of the Trinity are nothing like Emanations. Instead, the Persons are eternal, perfect, and changeless aspects of the One True God, Who is eternal, perfect, and changeless.

It's the word "person" that confuses Jews about the Trinity. (The word also confuses Moslems, whose teachings about Allah of the Koran are substantially equivalent to Jewish teachings about the God of the Torah.) In modern European languages, *person* has come to mean 'individual.' Thus, when Jews or Moslems hear us say, "God is one Nature in three Persons," they believe that we're saying that the One God is divided into three individuals, a statement that to them is absurd.

Let me give you an illustration. Picture three women, whom we may call Ann, Beth, and Claire. The three women share a common female nature. From a human point of view, we can truly say, "Ann, Beth, and Claire are three individuals who share one female nature." If we made the same kind of statement about the Father, the Son, and the Holy Spirit, though, we'd be guilty of a heresy called *tritheism*, teaching that there are three independently existing gods. Many Jews and Moslems believe that we're guilty of this heresy.

In ancient Latin, though, before *persona* ever meant 'individual,' it meant 'personality.' A persona was an outward expression of oneself that one showed the world. (*Persona* originally meant a mask that an actor wore in a play.) It is, of course, possible for one individual to show the world many personas.

Persona, though, is just a translation (a bad one, some say) of a term that was used in creeds (statement of belief) defining the Trinity. These creeds were written in Greek, which spoke of God's being one Nature in three *hypostases*. It shouldn't surprise you that the word *hypostasis*, being Greek, is difficult to define. Its root meaning is "that which stands below," and it can be translated by such English words as "foundation," "basis," "manifestation," or "reality."

What the Greek Fathers meant, though, by saying, "God is one Nature in three Hypostases" is just what I've been telling you, that the eternal, perfect, changeless God manifests Himself to creation in three eternal, perfect, changeless forms.

We believe, along with Jews, Kabbalists, Moslems, and Gnostics, that the ultimate God is an eternal, perfect, changeless unity of spirit. As such, He is beyond the power of human words to describe. It shouldn't surprise you, then, to learn that we have no words adequate to describe what the Persons or Hypostases of the Holy Trinity are. We can describe them only by analogy, using physical things to describe spiritual things. Sadly, analogy always falls short of the reality that it describes.

In catechism our Roman Catholic brothers and sisters learn what's probably the best analogy of the Holy Trinity ever devised, the analogy of water. Water may appear in three phases, ice, liquid, or water vapor, but, regardless of what phase it may be in, water's nature is unchanged.

Some have also compared the three Persons of the Trinity to three facets of a jewel. You can, if you want, use an ancient Latin meaning of *persona* and think of God as an actor who plays three roles in the cosmic play of Creator and Creation. Whatever you do, just keep in mind that the three Persons of God are beyond our power to describe, and that God is ultimately One.

As Trinitarian Christianity rejected the Gnostic concept of emanations, the Kabbalistic concept of spiritual Planes is foreign to Evangelical Christians. Some do accept a Roman Catholic teaching of seven heavens. Most Evangelicals, though, believe that there are just three heavens, the heaven of the clouds, the heaven of the stars, and the heaven of God's Throne Room. Of these the first two heavens are united to the earth as part of God's creation. God is directly active in creation today through the Person of the Holy Spirit.

Chapter Eight

A SERMON ON *YHWH*

You may've heard that Jews are forbidden to speak
God's Name, written as the Tetragrammaton, the four letters
YHWH. This, some scholars tell us, came from *Ehyeh*, "I Am,"
the Name by which God in the burning bush revealed Himself to
Moses. YHWH seems to mean something like "Eternal Being."

In ancient times Jews used the Name in everyday
speech. Shortly before the time of our Savior and Lord, though,
the rabbis grew concerned with the possibility that using the
Name in everyday speech carried the risk of violating God's
commandment, "Thou shalt not take the name of the LORD thy
God in vain." (Feel free to "Amen!" the rabbis on this point!)
The rabbis were also concerned with the activities of magicians
who were committing the ultimate act of black magic, conjuring
with the Name of the One True God.

Thus, the rabbis forbade public use of the Name. They
replaced it in speech with *Adonai*, 'My Lord.' When they wrote
the Name, they combined the consonants YHWH with the
vowels of Adonai. This, if someone in his or her ignorance read
it aloud, would produce a hybrid word that sounds like
"Jehovah."

It's sad to say that down through time many Evangelical
Christians, taken in by the rabbinical code, have used the name
Jehovah as if it were truly God's Name. They've done so on the
authority of the King James Bible, whose translators sometimes
chose to put the word "Jehovah" into print. (More often, they
chose to print the Name as LORD, as I did above.) God's
Name has never been Jehovah.

Despite the rabbis' best efforts, a scholarly reconstruction of the correct pronunciation of YHWH has become common knowledge. Since it is, I'll give it here, along with a plea for you never to speak it.

Scholars have been able to reconstruct the correct pronunciation of the Name from the writings of Greco-Egyptian magicians, Gnostics, and early Church Fathers, who wrote the Name down phonetically in Greek letters. Most commonly these formed a sequence of five vowels: *iota, alpha, omicron, upsilon, eta*. These, scholars say, represent the Hebrew word *Yahweh*.

I've noticed that, in Evangelical Christian meetings, new preachers and teachers like to impress their congregations or classes by calling God Yahweh. Why do I say that they shouldn't call God Yahweh?

I say so because the original text of the New Testament, the sole rule of faith and practice for Evangelical Christians, was written in Greek, which, as I said above, is perfectly capable of transliterating the Name from Hebrew. Nonetheless, the Name nowhere appears in the New Testament. Instead, you'll notice that, when Christ and His Apostles spoke of God Eternal, they called him *kurios*, 'Lord.' Clearly, they were following the rabbinical teaching to replace the Name in speech with 'Lord' and never to write it down in a pronounceable form.

The New Testament gives no authority for a Christian to speak the Name. Instead, the New Testament tells the believer to follow the example of Christ and His Apostles, not to be "puffed up" in knowledge, and not to give needless offense to Jews. Thus, Christians should avoid saying the Name.

Chapter Nine

A SERMON ON *SHEKHINAH*

My Evangelical brothers and sisters may've been confused by how I've used the term *Shekhinah*. This is a term that Evangelical Christians often use to describe the Glory of God, His fire and light that appear in theophanies, or earthly manifestations, of God's heavenly nature.

We believe that Jesus Christ, God's Son, One with the Father and the Holy Spirit in the Blessed Trinity, is the ultimate theophany, the incarnation of the Shekhinah, God's Glory. Jesus, of course, in His human body, was male. Thus, it may surprise my fellow Evangelicals to learn that many Jews nowadays consider the Shekhinah female.

First, you need to know that the word *shekhinah* never appears in Hebrew Scripture in reference to God. There the term **kavod,** 'glory,' announces God's fire and light appearing in the world.

Shekhinah, which means 'tent,' or 'dwelling-place,' was first applied to God by the rabbis who gave rise to the Talmud. They used the term to express their wonder at God's light staying with us in a fallen world. In using the term *shekhinah*, the rabbis didn't intend to imply that God is of one gender or the other. They simply used the ordinary word for 'tent.' Evangelical Christian scholars who popularized the term *shekhinah* were following Talmudic usage.

The early rabbis believed, as we believe, that the eternal, transcendent God has no gender. The eternal God, Who is uncreated and undivided, can't be described in terms of that which is created and can be distinguished from an opposite.

The Hebrew language, though, like modern French and Spanish, classifies everything as either masculine or feminine. The set of nouns and pronouns for God consisted for the most part of masculine words. Thus, the early rabbis, like us, kept the Scriptural use of *He* to refer to God.

They, like us, though, believe that it's **blasphemy** (slander of what's holy) to say that the transcendent God actually has anything like male or female physical traits. To do so would be to confuse the Creator, Who is eternal and changeless, with His temporary and changeable creation.

Thus, the word *shekhinah*, which is grammatically feminine, implies no more about God's sexuality, God forbid, than the word *He* does. It's superstitious and heretical to say that God Eternal is either male or female.

To be inclusive, you'd do better not to use the word *She*, but to point out that the word *He* is just a tradition based on grammar. To call God *She* carries the risk of bringing into pure monotheism pagan concepts of a separate, changeable goddess in contrast with the eternal, changeless One. To call God *It* would deny His personality; to call Him *they,* to deny His ultimate Unity.

The Kabbalists agree with the early rabbis and us as far as Ein Sof is concerned. The Kabbalists, though, believe that sexuality arose when God poured His light into the vessels of the Ten Planes, and these refracted it as stained glass lends its color to light that passes through it. On the basis of Biblical descriptions of relations between men and women, Kabbalists described higher manifestations of God as masculine, but the lowest as feminine.

You'll learn more of the relations between the higher manifestations of God and the Shekhinah as this book goes on. In any case, though, the Kabbalists, who believe that God directly created the Hebrew language, believe that He made the word *shekhinah* feminine to show us that the Divine Light that dwells among us is female.

Please be careful, then, of how you use the word *shekhinah*. If you're in an Evangelical Christian Bible study, use the word freely. If, though, you're sharing your faith with a Jewish or New Age friend, be aware of the danger that you're communicating to them something that you didn't mean to say. Misunderstanding arises when you use a word that means one thing to you and a different thing to your friend. If you use the word *Shekhinah*, he or she will think that you're calling God female!

Chapter Ten

THE FALL ACCORDING TO KABBALAH

Kabbalists teach, as I told earlier, that Creation began when Ein Sof contracted to form vessels, then filled them with divine light. The filling of the vessels ended in a disaster called **shevirah**, or 'the breaking of the vessels." The light was too much for the vessels to hold. They shattered, and divine light became scattered as sparks trapped in broken vessels.

(You'll sometimes see the word **kelipot** used to describe these. This word, like most Hebrew words written in English, may appear in many different ways. Non-Jews who use Kabbalah for magical purposes tend to write *kelipot* as *qellipot,* and Kabbalah as *Qabalah.* As I'll explain later, if your teen-aged son is engaged in *qellipotic* activities, he's mixed up in black magic.)

God then created Adam to repair the broken vessels and gather up the scattered sparks so that creation could be restored to God's vision of glory. Adam, though, fell into sin, and died.

(To make matters clear, I should mention that the Adam to whom I'm referring here is **Adam ha-Rishon,** the earthly Adam, not Adam Kadmon, the primeval Adam of the Ten Planes, who expresses what we can know of God. Adam ha-Rishon is an earthly expression of Adam Kadmon. Only the earthly Adam sinned, though, of course, the heavenly Adam was involved in the *Shevirah.)*

The Bible attributes Adam's fall to accepting forbidden fruit from Eve, the wife whom God had formed from Adam so that she was flesh of his flesh and bone of his bone, one flesh with him. The fall of one component of this two who were one entailed the fall of the other.

Kabbalah tells a number of other stories of Adam's fall. These tend to involve his committing sexual sin with a she-demon named Lilith, who was the fallen Eve of an earlier creation that God had destroyed. (You'll find more on earlier creations in the books that I've listed in Bibliography. Any discussion of earlier creations lies beyond this book's scope.) In any case, Adam's fall was a reflection on the earth of the breaking of the vessels in the heavenly Planes.

We and the Kabbalists have different views on what it means that Adam died. Before we can consider, though, what Adam's death meant, we need to ask a thorny question, "Where do souls come from?"

Theologians have three answers to this question:

ONE: God directly creates a new soul for each person who is conceived.

Some Evangelical Christians accept this answer. Others, though, point out that, for this to be true, God would have to be directly responsible for sending a perfect soul into a fallen world where that soul is doomed to fall, too.

TWO: Our souls come to us from our parents.

Most Evangelical Christians accept this answer. One can ask, though, that, if it's true, isn't our sinful nature passed to us genetically, and couldn't we save humanity from sin through genetic engineering?

THREE: Souls are pre-existent, and come to us from the heavens with experiences.

This is the answer that Kabbalists accept. They share it with Hindus, Buddhists, Mormons, and Scientologists.

Jesus dealt with this question in the account of the man born blind, about whom our Lord's disciples asked, "Who sinned, this man, or his parents, that he was born blind?" Although Jesus didn't directly reject the pre-existence of human souls, his answer that neither the man's sin nor his parents' was responsible for his blindness has led most Christian theologians to reject the soul's pre-existence.

Kabbalists, though, accept this, along with, as you'll learn, the kindred doctrine of reincarnation. In Kabbalistic thinking, the souls of every human being are bound up in a single, original soul that came to Adam ha-Rishon, the first man created in the Garden of Eden. This soul reached Adam through *Shekhinah*. Thus, Kabbalists see a special relationship and connection between every human being and Adam, and also between every human being and *Shekhinah*.

Now we're ready to look at what Adam's death meant.

We teach that Adam **died spiritually** (became separated from God) as soon as he sinned, and that his physical death was a delayed consequence of his spiritual death.

Kabbalists teach that Adam had a "supersoul" consisting of all of humanity's spiritual energy. When Adam rebelled against God, Adam's soul was shattered into "mini-souls" that would become **incarnate** (be born into human flesh) in his descendants. Adam's death, therefore, was the shattering of the soul with which God had created him.

Oddly enough, from highly different perspectives, both Kabbalists and many Evangelical Christians have come to believe in **original sin**, the concept that "In Adam's fall, we sinned all." We believe that each person is born with a sinful nature that comes from one's parents. Kabbalists believe that each of us is directly responsible for Adam's sin because every one of us has part of Adam's soul in him or her.

The Kabbalists paint a bleak picture of the Fall. At the end of it:

- creation is broken
- God's light is scattered
- we're trapped on the dark side of broken vessels
- Adam's soul is shattered
- the Shekhinah, which came into the world for humanity's sake, is trapped here in exile from the higher, masculine parts of God

Both we and the Kabbalists agree on a key point:

- creation and humanity are fallen and need redemption.

Chapter Eleven

REDEMPTION ACCORDING TO KABBALAH

Fixing the World

We believe that God sent His Son, our Savior and Lord Jesus Christ, into the world

- to live the sinless life that we could not
- to die to pay the penalty for sin that we could not
- to rise from death to give us the eternal life of the Father
- to ascend to the heavenly throne room to build us a home there
- to come again from there to take us home as His Bride

Kabbalists tell a different story from ours. According to them, Adam's descendants still have his original mission to put the shattered creation back together. This mission is expressed in the Hebrew phrase ***tikkun olam***, 'fixing the world.'

One fixes the world by performing works of righteousness. Gentiles can help this process to some degree by following the light of creation and conscience in what the rabbis call the seven **Noachide** (pertaining to Noah) **laws**. Briefly put, these forbid idolatry, murder, blasphemy, adultery, stealing, and eating the flesh of a living animal, and command establishing courts of justice to enforce the other laws.

It falls to Jews, though, to be the major players in redemption by following the Law of Moses. This consists, in the Talmudic reckoning, of 613 distinct commands. Each of these plays an indispensable role in the world's redemption. Most of these commands are negative commandments ("Thou shalt not"). Violation of these plunges the world deeper into spiritual darkness. The rest of the commands are positive commandments ("Thou shalt"). Keeping these raises the world into spiritual light.

Kabbalists teach, though, that it isn't enough just to perform the commandments. To be truly effective in changing the world, a commandment must be performed in *kavanah.* This means, with the intention of pleasing God, not in view of any earthly reward. Only actions performed in purity of spirit can help purge the world of evil. A commandment performed with bad intentions may do nothing to heal the world, or may even make it worse.

Once, Jews performed the commandments as members of a community centered on the temple in Jerusalem. According to Rabbi Luria, though, God allowed the destruction of the temple and the *Diaspora* (dispersion, or scattering) of the Jews from the Holy Land so that they could lead the way in healing creation throughout the world. Seen in light of Lurianic teaching, the *Aliyah* (ascent), or return of the Jews to the Holy Land, is a sign of Messiah's immanent coming.

(Many Evangelical Christians, though for reasons different from those of Kabbalists, also interpret the regathering of the Jews to the Holy Land as a sign of the Messiah's coming. In our case, though, the coming for which we look is the Second Coming, the return of Jesus Christ to the earth in power and glory to overcome evil and set up the Millennial Kingdom of global peace and righteousness. It's common, both among Kabbalistic Jews and Evangelical Christians, to see the Messianic reign as centered on a rebuilt temple in Jerusalem.)

Kabbalists teach that every righteous act frees a spark of light from the shattered shell that imprisons it, and raises that spark to God. Thus, each act of righteousness brings closer the coming of Messiah. In his day

- the scattered light will be regathered
- the broken vessels will be repaired
- Adam's soul will be reunited
- the Shekhinah will be rejoined to God

Mystical Marriage

Readers of Kabbalistic literature learn that sex plays a major role in Jewish mysticism and especially in healing the world. Nothing is more open to being misunderstood than the role of sex in religion. Thus, I must speak both clearly and carefully of sexual mysticism in Kabbalah and what it implies for Evangelical Christians.

In Evangelical Christian teaching, marriage is one of two states in which God has permitted humans to live, the other being celibacy. It's up to each of us, with God's guidance, to determine the state in which we should live. In general, we shouldn't think one state better than the other. We believe that God has called some persons to be celibate, and others to be married, for the sake of the work that God has called each person to do.

Celibacy is a word often confused with *chastity* in common use. *Celibacy* means 'abstaining from marriage'; *chastity*, 'having sexual relations only in a state of purity.' Every Christian should be chaste, even though not every Christian need be celibate.

As Evangelical Christians read the Bible, pure sexual relations are possible only in a marriage of one man and one woman committed to each other for life. A Christian can be sexually active, but chaste, only in marriage. Evangelical Christians generally follow the apostolic teaching that partners in a marriage shouldn't deprive each other of sexual relations, which should be interrupted only for a special occasion such as an extended season of prayer.

Orthodox Jews believe, as we believe, that chaste sexual relations are possible only in marriage. It's not surprising that this is so, as the apostles who set down the New Testament teachings on sex and marriage were once Orthodox Jews! Unlike us, though, Orthodox Jews believe that marriage is preferable to celibacy. In Orthodox Jewish eyes, celibacy is an inferior, even sinful, state in which the celibate person rejects the blessing of sexuality, which God created and called good.

In Orthodox Jewish eyes, each person has an obligation to enjoy, and bless God for, all of the good things that He has created. Thus, it surprises Evangelical Christians to learn that every Jew must follow the commandment to drink alcohol!

Not to do so would deprive him or her of a good thing that God created, and of the opportunity to say the blessing, "Blessed art Thou, Lord our God, King of the Universe, Who hast created the fruit of the vine." We, though, generally see the use of alcohol as a potential source of evil, the proven cost of which to individuals and society far outweighs any blessings that it might bestow on us.

Thus, Orthodox Judaism, as a rule, teaches that each person should marry and enjoy regular sexual relations whenever both partners in the marriage are pure. 'Pure' in this case means that each partner is, not only ritually pure in terms of the Law of Moses, but also free of negative emotions such as anger and jealousy that poison a marriage.

Kabbalah, building on Orthodox teachings, goes on to say that the commandments to marry and to enjoy sexual relations in marriage are two of the most powerful positive commandments, keeping which can heal the world. Kabbalists teach that a marriage of committed Jews is an earthly reflection of the heavenly marriage of the Planes *Shekhinah* and *Tif'eret.* On the principle of "As above, so below," of which I'll say more later, Kabbalists teach that sexual relations in a state of purity in marriage encourage the union of *Shekhinah* and *Tif'eret* and bring closer the appearance of Messiah.

You may come across Kabbalistic sacred sexuality in terms of "waters above" and "waters below." The pure sexual union of a Jewish man and wife "raises the waters below," which draw down the waters above, the union of *Tif'eret* and *Shekhinah.* Sexual relations, in Kabbalistic thinking, are especially effective in drawing down the waters above on Sabbath Eve, when *Shekhinah,* as Queen of the Sabbath, is symbolically married to *Tif'eret.*

The concept of a mystical marriage isn't original to Kabbalah. This concept appears in Jewish Scripture, in which imagery of marriage and even of sexual relations describe the relation between the LORD and Israel.

The Apostles Paul and John transferred this imagery to the relation between Christ and His Bride, the Church. Christian writers have generally been more cautious than Kabbalists about using sexual imagery to describe the relation between God and humans. Still, it is permissible for Christians to speak of sex in marriage as a type of the heavenly communion of Christ with His Bride, as long as Christian married couples don't believe that, when they're having sex, they're saving the world.

On one point, though, both Evangelical Christians and Kabbalists are in firm agreement: wrongful sexual relations are a powerful force for plunging the world into spiritual darkness!

Getting a Second Chance

It's in terns of redemption that ***gilgul***, the Kabbalistic concept of reincarnation, arises. It's impossible in one lifetime for each of Adam's souls to complete its mission of observing every one of Moses' commands. Thus, at the death of one's body, one's soul returns to ***Guf***, the Well of Souls, to be reborn in the world's next age.

There are six ages, each corresponding to one of the days of creation of Genesis One. Each age is a thousand years long, "for," as it is written, "a day with the Lord is as a thousand years." At the end of the sixth age, the Well of Souls will be empty, and Messiah will come.

(I should note here that many Evangelical Christians, though they reject reincarnation, have accepted the teaching of a world that lasts six thousand years from its creation. On the basis of Gematria-like calculations of when the sixth thousand-year day will end, some Evangelical Christians have made precise predictions of when the events surrounding the Second Coming will begin.

The recent past is littered with predictions that have been wrong. Their failure should remind us of our Lord's teaching, "No one knows the day of My coming except the Father in heaven.")

It's controversial to what, if any, extent the Kabbalistic concept of reincarnation is due to the Hindu/Buddhist concept, which had spread to the Mediterranean world by the time of the early Jewish mystics. Both concepts share the theme of a second chance to deal with events of a prior life. In Eastern religion, though, the second chance is largely negative; one is working off the consequences of wrongs committed before one's birth. In Kabbalah, the second chance is positive; one is doing good deeds to speed Messiah's coming.

Both Eastern religion and Kabbalah, though, seem to predict the disappearance of personality once the cycle of reincarnation is over. In Eastern religion, the consciousness of a person who through righteousness escapes the wheel of rebirth merges with the universal consciousness as a drop of water merges with the sea.

In Kabbalah, the shattered parts of Adam ha-Rishon's soul reunite to reform the original "supersoul." This, in turn, achieves mystical union with the Plane *Binah*, through which it will attain union with Wisdom, Crown, and ultimately Ein Sof. In both cases, what is individual vanishes; only what is universal remains.

In contrast with Eastern religion and Kabbalah, Christian Scripture seems to teach persistence of the glorified individual believer in a glorified Church. Scripture speaks of this persistence as the believer's being a member of the Bride, a stone in the New Jerusalem, and a pillar in the Temple in which God will dwell with us forever through the Holy Spirit. Still, even Christian Scripture teaches that in the end God will be all in all.

Whenever any of us, whether Eastern religionist, Kabbalist, or Evangelical Christian, though, speaks of life beyond death, he or she should display the humility to recognize that what lies there is something beyond our earthly experience. We no more have words in human languages to describe life beyond death than we have to describe God Eternal.

Chapter Twelve

A SERMON ON WORKS OF RIGHTEOUSNESS

It's common for outsiders to accuse us who believe in salvation by grace through faith of **antinomianism**. In simple terms, this is 'being against the Law.' (It never ceases to amaze me how many terms theologians have made up to denounce those who differ from them.)

Antinomianism, broadly put, is the sin of believing that we can live however we want to after we're saved. Some falsely accuse us of saying, "Let's sin all that we want to on Saturday because we'll be forgiven on Sunday!" (The same false accusation is made of Roman Catholics in respect of confession.)

It's true that Christians are freed of the need to keep Moses' law so that we can keep a law of love in our Savior and Lord Jesus Christ. Love in Christ, though, isn't just a feeling, but is belief put into action through works of righteousness. Ephesians 2:8-10, the passage that most clearly proclaims salvation by grace through faith, ends in the teaching that we're saved for the sake of our doing works that God has prepared for us to do.

Good works are

- a service of duty that we owe to the One Who bought us out of the slave-market of sin
- a service of love that we owe to the One Who loved us enough to die for us
- a natural response to the Holy Spirit living within us
- a means of bringing blessings to this world and earning rewards in the World to Come

- a means of adorning the Body of Christ as the Bride for whom the Bridegroom will return

Let's, then, never grow weary of doing good works, but let's keep in mind that we aren't the Savior, Jesus is! It's through His sacrifice, the shedding of His blood on the tree, that we're saved from our spiritual darkness, it's through the presence and power of His Holy Spirit within us that we can do works of righteousness, and it will be through His return, not through our efforts, that evil will at last be overcome forever.

Chapter Thirteen

KABBALISTIC MAGIC

We've learned that much spiritual energy, in terms of scattered sparks of God's light, is lying around. We've also learned that the Hebrew letters hold the power of creation. Can Kabbalists use this energy and this power to work wonders?

They say, "Yes!" In fact, many Kabbalists say that every righteous act is an act of *theurgy*, an influencing of the heavenly through the earthly, because it raises a spark of God's fallen light back to the higher Planes.

Artificial Life

On the basis of "As above, so below," the magical principle that everything in the higher Planes corresponds with something on the earth, Kabbalists who practice magic claim to have done works far mightier than just raising sparks. The ultimate work is the creation of the *Golem*, an artificial human being brought to life from inanimate matter. This work requires prolonged study of *Sefer Yetzirah* and lengthy recitations of combinations and permutations of divine names while the reciters are ritually pure.

In Kabbalistic lore a golem's creation was entirely an act of meditation on God as Creator. The virtue of creating a golem would be lost if its creators tried to do anything useful with it in the created world. Jewish legend, though, says that in the Middle Ages rabbis created Golems to guard persecuted Jewish communities from those who called themselves Children of Light, but did works of darkness.

We've all learned the story of the Golem from two adaptations of it. The first is Mary Shelley's **Frankenstein**. In this early science-fiction novel she updated the tale of the Golem by replacing Kabbalistic magic with electricity as the means to animate inanimate matter. Dr. Frankenstein's work, which stemmed from sinful pride that took no responsibility for what it had produced, ended in tragedy.

Mary Shelley's monster, which destroys its creator, differs from the legendary Golem, which protects its creators. Kabbalists saw human use of God's power to create life as good; Mary Shelley, as a potential source of evil. One wonders whether modern genetic engineering, applied to human beings, will result in the Golem, and whether it'll resemble Frankenstein's monster more than it resembles the Golem of the Kabbalists.

The second story of the Golem with which we're familiar is the story of Superman. He was imagined by a pair of Jewish comic-book writers who'd grown up in an ultra-Orthodox community and were familiar with Jewish legends. In fact, Superman's Kryptonian name, *Kal-El,* is Hebrew for 'All-God'! Superman, in contrast with Frankenstein's monster, embodies the Jewish ideal of the Golem, a selfless defender of a righteous community from evildoers.

Lawful and Unlawful Magic

The white magic of which Kabbalistic magicians approve, they call "magic of the right-hand path." This refers to the convention of drawing the Ten Spiritual Planes as a man or a tree. On this drawing Mercy appears as the right hand. Magic, so Kabbalists say, that flows from on high through the right hand produces healing and happiness, and is intended for the benefit of the magician, the community, and God.

Kabbalah, though, also holds much potential for black magic, intended for dominating others and making them suffer. This potential arose through the breaking of the vessels, the fall of the angels associated with them, and the arising of demons.

Black magic is called "magic of the left-hand path" because it flows through Strength or Judgment, the Plane drawn as the left hand. Strength or Judgment unbalanced by Mercy, Kabbalists say, results in oppression that justifies itself in terms of keeping order. Mercy, though, unbalanced by Strength or Judgment, results in toleration of evil through inability to resist it.

Fans of *Star Trek: The Original Series* saw Kabbalistic teachings on Mercy and Judgment acted out in "The Enemy Within." In this episode a transporter accident divides Captain Kirk into two bodies, one dominated by Mercy, the other by Strength.

The Strength Kirk is decisive, but totally selfish and brutal. The Mercy Kirk is compassionate, but lacks strength of will to make hard decisions needed to rescue his men, trapped on a hostile planet. Only the reunion of Mercy and Strength lets Kirk save the day. And you thought that it was all just science fiction!

Disembodied Spirits

Some branches of Kabbalah see the possibility of humans being possessed by wandering souls. These are pieces of the primal Adam's shattered soul that are seeking to work out some lack in a previous life.

Oddly enough to our Evangelical Christian way of thinking, Kabbalah teaches that sometimes being possessed can be a good thing. In times of crisis, a type of wandering soul called an **ibbur** can come to you. The *ibbur* is a spark of Adam's soul that has failed to fulfill a certain commandment in its previous lifetimes. By helping you fulfill that commandment, the *ibbur* can fulfill its own obligation to the law.

You might also, though, run into an evil spirit called a **dybbuk**. This is a spark of Adam's soul that has become so imbued with sin that it can no longer be allowed to reincarnate. The *dybbuk* seeks a living human being as a vessel through which it can express its evil. A *dybbuk's* victim suffers terribly. A *dybbuk* can be exorcized only by a *baal shem*, a Kabbalah master who knows the secret names of God.

A *dybbuk* in some ways resembles the demons that Christ and His apostles cast out of victims in the Holy Land. Evangelical Christians differ on whether such demons are active in the world today. Those who believe that such demons are active may seek to cast them out with prayer, fasting, and the laying on of hands. Others, though, believe that demonic possession is a phenomenon associated with Christ's physical presence in the world, and thus does not occur today.

Protective Magic

Because of the possibility of magic of the left-hand path, Kabbalists see a need for protective magic. They teach, as we teach, that the greatest protection against spiritual evil is studying God's Word and doing God's works of prayer, fellowship with other believers, and service to those in need of help.

Kabbalists, though, may also see a need for amulets, protective jewels that embody the power of Hebrew letters or other items that can channel spiritual energy. Of such amulets the one with which you're likely most familiar is the red string. This is supposed to protect the wearer against a form of black magic called "the evil eye," empowered by an enemy's envy and jealousy.

The red string has a Biblical origin in three separate events. The string first appears in the account of the birth of the Patriarch Judah's twin sons, in which the string was tied around the firstborn's foot to distinguish him from his brother.

The string next appears in the account of the harlot Rahab, who tied it to her house as a sign to Hebrew warriors to spare her household in the sack of Jericho.

The string last appears in the sacrifice of the scapegoat, to whose horn it was tied before he was taken into the wilderness. According to Talmudic tradition, the string turned white if God accepted that sacrifice.

Thus, the red string is supposed to convey to its wearer the blessing of the firstborn, the protection given to Rahab, and the redemption of the scapegoat.

We, as Evangelical Christians, should have nothing to do with ritual magic or amulets. We must follow the teachings of Moses' Law and of Scripture in general, which forbids believers to practice divination, traffic with spirits, or raise the dead through necromantic rites as the witch of Endor raised the Prophet Samuel.

We have no need of amulets. Since we have the indwelling presence of the Holy Spirit and membership in the Body of Christ, with our Savior and Lord as its head, what spiritual evil can touch us as long as we keep our eyes on Jesus? All of our spiritual needs are met by the Blood of the Lamb, which saves us and makes us clean in God's sight.

BIBLIOGRAPHY

NOTE: The following bibliography is not intended to be either comprehensive or scholarly. It is simply a list of the books that I've read to prepare to write the book that you hold in your hand. I'm providing you with this list so that you can read further in the books that have guided me in learning what I know of Kabbalah.

Dan, Joseph, ed., Kiener, Ronald C., transl., Idel, Moshe, *The Early Kabbalah,* Paulist Press, 1986.

Goldwag, Arthur, *The Beliefnet Guide to Kabbalah,* Doubleday: Three Leaves Press, 2005.

Kaplan, Aryeh, transl., *The Bahir,* Weiser Books, 1997.

Kaplan, Aryeh, transl., *Sefer Yetzirah, The Book of Creation: In Theory and Practice, Revised Edition,* Weiser Books, 1997.

Laitman, Rav Michael, PhD, *Kabbalah for Beginners: A Beginner's Guide to the Hidden Wisdom,* Laitman Kabbalah Publishers, 2005.

Matt, Daniel C., ed., *The Essential Kabbalah: The Heart of Jewish Mysticism,* HarperSanFrancisco, 1996.

Matt, Daniel Chanan, transl., *Zohar, the Book of Enlightenment,* Paulist Press, 1983.

Scholem, Gershom, *Kabbalah,* Meridian, 1978.

Scholem, Gershom, *On the Kabbalah and Its Symbolism,* Schocken Books, 1996.

Scholem, Gershom, *On the Mystical Shape of the Godhead: Basic Concepts in the Kabbalah,* Schocken Books, 1991.

Scholem, Gershom, ed. *Zohar, The Book of Splendor: Basic Readings from the Kabbalah,* Schocken Books, 1977.

Zalman, Schneur, *Likutei Amoraim: Tanya,* Brooklyn: "Kehot" Publication Society, 1981.

www.ingramcontent.com/pod-product-compliance
Lightning Source LLC
Chambersburg PA
CBHW032035090426
42741CB00006B/822